MEDICAL ETHICS AND HUMAN LIFE

MEDICAL ETHICS
AND
HUMAN LIFE

David Braine

SECOND EDITION

WIPF & STOCK · Eugene, Oregon

Wipf and Stock Publishers
199 W 8th Ave, Suite 3
Eugene, OR 97401

Medical Ethics and Human Life
By Braine, David
Copyright©1983 by Braine, David
ISBN 13: 978-1-5326-7761-8
Publication date 12/12/2018
Previously published by Palladio Press, 1983

Preface

When I wrote the first version of this essay (in 1979), I deliberately cast my view more widely than the area of principal controversy at that time (i.e. abortion), and set myself to consider the principles governing all cases of the wrongful taking of human life, whether one's own (suicide) or another person's ('murder'), including notably the case of voluntary euthanasia which involves both, and also cases affecting the handicapped and enfeebled, whether before birth, new-born, or in mature years. Always my concern was with deliberate or planned action, whether by individual or society, not with cases of action 'when the balance of one's mind is disturbed'.

Since that time, the importance of such wider consideration has become more evident, as cases of infanticide in paediatrics, cases affecting the handicapped, and questions of euthanasia, have all come into public controversy. In regard to all of them, my anxiety has been to *explain*, and *make clear*, not to dogmatise. In particular, my anxiety has been to *explain* how the recognition of the sanctity of life is an intimate and necessary consequence of the basic understanding of God and man, and of God's role in the creation and upholding of persons in existence, integral to both Judaism and Christianity.

The citations from the early Christian Fathers merely confirm what is already evident in the general Biblical understanding of man, as well as in Rabbinic tradition. But these citations are striking for their freshness, as much at variance with pagan as with any modern morality. I am very grateful for the help of Mr Anthony Schmitz in assembling these citations, utilising existing translations with some limited modernisation and correction where this seemed necessary, as well as for enormous help and encouragement in regard to the rest of the project.

Foreword to the Second Edition

The demand for the first edition of this work has made clear the need for such an exposition of the underlying basic *principles* affecting medical and paramedical workers' approach to human life. It is vital to avoid thinking of human life as, like a hotel, to be valued only according to its 'quality' or amenity value, rather than as having some intrinsic worth to be respected for its own sake. The extent to which this 'quality of life' way of thinking has come to dominate the deliberations of public committees and the discussions conducted amongst doctors themselves is steadily on the increase and its beginnings are well documented in Part One of *Euthanasia and Clinical Practice* published in 1982 by the Linacre Centre. This report (available from The Linacre Centre, 60 Grove End Road, London NW8 9NH) in its careful separate examination of the cases of the newborn, the handicapped, the elderly, as well as of the cases of terminal and intensive care, provides in Part One and Part Four a useful application in detail of the guiding principles my booklet indicated in only briefest outline. Part Four of the former also very usefully indicates the large extent of the proper right to refuse disproportionate care, i.e. the extent to which refusal of care can be non-suicidal and non-euthanasiast.

In the booklet in its final form I was more concerned with euthanasia than with abortion. However, the development of screening techniques and the application of eugenic principles to the treatment of the unborn and the newborn, for example in the ever more extensive screening of foetuses and the practice of amniocentesis, bring a new urgency to the application of the principle of respect for life as a gift to the unborn and the newborn as well as to the elderly and enfeebled. The practice of any pruning of the human race when in the womb or newly born will lead inexorably step by step to a willingness to prune the human race of the more handicapped, the more mentally retarded or disordered and those enfeebled by ill health and age.

Against this tendency every human being needs to make a stand in the name of humanity itself.

CONTENTS

Introduction

I write in this essay as a Christian addressing fellow-Christians and all others who share with them belief in God or a religious sense of the value of human life.

The sanctity of human life has already been brought into question in our society in the case of abortion, and we may expect it soon to be brought into wider question in respect of euthanasia, including some cases of infanticide. In this situation the Christian can easily find himself pushed into a false position. Because he wishes to commend his position to our secular society, he is liable to emphasise only those objections to these practices (in fact, very powerful objections) which it seems ought in reason to appeal to the secular humanist and the utilitarian as well as to the Christian. But in doing this he is liable to find that he has little influence, for two reasons. Firstly, those to whom he is speaking are in fact not chiefly moved by general moral considerations whether of the long-term happiness of the greater number or of any other kind, but rather by (a) the desire simply to give parents, relatives, women pregnant with child, and any others who present themselves as clients, what they want or what they ask for without seeming illiberal or uncooperative and also by (b) the pressures which result from the absence of the motivation or economic resources to direct more time and effort to alternative and more human responses to the situations in which people seek abortion or euthanasia. Secondly, the Christian has so fallen in with secular man's ways of thinking in these areas that he has ceased to be conscious of the peculiarly strong ground he has, precisely as a Christian and as a believer in God, for being opposed to these practices, and as a result has ceased to provide effective witness even to his fellow-Christians.

Therefore, while conscious of the strong non-religious reasons there are for objecting to these practices, I propose in this paper

9

to concentrate upon the way this matter should appear to a Christian or to anyone who shares a Christian type of belief about God and man. I shall begin by describing the traditional Christian position, and will then consider the reasons for it, that is the inner connections between this position and the rest of Christian belief, so that we can see that the Christian attitude is not built upon appeal to the authority of merely isolated dogmas or texts but springs intimately from the basic understanding of God and man at the heart of Christianity and Judaism. I shall then deal with the chief commonly felt objection to the traditional position, and then finally pass some comments on the form which witness of Christian to non-Christian, and fellow-Christian to fellow-Christian should take.

I

The Traditional Position

For the whole of Christian history until appreciably after 1900, so far as we can trace it, there was virtually complete unanimity amongst Christians, evangelical, catholic, orthodox, that, unless at the direct command of God, it was in all cases wrong directly to take innocent human life. Abortion and infanticide were grouped together as early as the writing called the *Didache* which comes from the first century after the crucifixion. These deeds were grouped with murder in that those committing or co-operating in them were, when penitent, still excluded from Communion for ten years by early Councils. Suicide and, by implication, voluntary euthanasia have been regarded as much more grave if or in so far as they expressed ultimate despair in the person to be killed, in addition to the wrongfulness of the killing. All were regarded as grave wrongs, acts both inhuman and irreligious. On the other hand, while co-operation of Christians in war was in early times dubious, secular authorities were not regarded as wrong in killing those acting against public order (as in police-type action) or in exacting punishment. The absolute bar was against the deliberate taking of *innocent* life, not in the sense of sinless life, but in the sense of life which was *innocens* (not harming), life not presently wilfully co-operating in or planning grave harm, and not regarded as guilty of this in the past so as to be open to punishment. Nor was there an absolute bar against just any action which might foreseeably issue, certainly or probably, in loss of life, whether one's own or another's, but rather against action directly aimed at this, or directly choosing it even if only as a means to somethig else. We may note that this strictness constituted one of the most dramatic identifiable

11

differences between Christian morality and pagan, Greek or Roman, morality. Pagan morality commonly countenanced infanticide and suicide (as well as allowing things like vicarious punishment and relatively indiscriminate killing in war and in dealing with civil disturbances).

However, whether in the area of methods in war, or of the practice of medicine, we are today confronted with the question, whether this norm of *absolute respect for innocent life* should stand, or, whether (on the grounds either of supposed social necessity or of compassion) it should sometimes be waived. In face of such questioning we can proceed in two ways. (i) We can appeal to the authority of *tradition,* i.e., of that which has been *handed down to us* (*traditum*) as belonging to Divinely Revealed Law, whether in this we appeal to the witness of the Church or of the Bible; or (ii) we can seek to go deeper and enquire into the inner connection between the extraordinary unanimity amongst Christians in the past and their general understanding of the relation between God and the world.

Now, when Christian positions are under attack, it is often inviting and sometimes right simply to batten down the hatches, holding on to the tradition received without wavering, amidst confusion intellectual or otherwise in the minds of oneself or of others. It is largely in this way that Christianity has survived under Islamic and Communist regimes. Our own society is very intolerant of any such battening down the hatches approach, because, while theoretically tolerant of non-conformists, it preaches open discussion, even in contexts where the conditions of discussion are loaded against the non-conformist. It is said that brain-washing proceeds by getting people into states of maximum tiredness, and then landing them in situations of intellectual complication and, if possible, conflicting obligation and personal involvement with the brain-washers; and that in these circumstances the best resistance to the process is put up by those who refuse to get involved with their captors, and especially those who refuse to get involved in argument. However, while individuals not involved in the personal problems which give rise to the demand for abortion or euthanasia may adopt this policy of not getting involved, counsellors and doctors confronted with patients or clients, and involved in complex relations with their seniors and juniors, cannot. The trainee doctor or social worker, and indeed their mentors also, are subjected to extremes of tiredness, argument and conflicting obligation, a direct analogue of the brain-washing situation. Since the option of not arguing or discussing is very difficult to follow in respect of their patients, clients or juniors, there is an urgent need to supplement the appeal to authority (which is useless except to those who accept the same authority, whether Church or Bible) with understanding. And only such understanding can rescue those who would prefer to batten down the hatches from appearing stuck with somewhat arbitary private interpretations of authority—presenting to their non-Christian associates the image either of arbitrary points of rigidity, or else of peculiar and ill-explained let-outs. So, while the Christian does better to resort to authority than to situation-ethics (which seems the exact recipe for openness to brain-washing), and has no magic which puts understanding, as it were, at his command (he sometimes has to move forward in faith amidst darkness), nonetheless he should desire understanding, and, if this paper has any value, it is in providing a service towards this.

Why then should these acts have been regarded as not only inhuman, but also irreligious?

II

Taking Innocent Life: an Irreligious Act

The human being is, according to Christian understanding, a being made by God for relationship with Himself, a personal relationship capable or remaining even after the perishing and death of the body, whether this relationship be one of faith and love, or whether it be one of rejecting God's grace. The human being, on this view, is a being whose existence transcends the merely physical and biological, and is outside the powers of the merely material and biological, either to bring into existence, or to maintain in existence.

Modern man, however, is apt to misunderstand this teaching. He is apt to think of the Universe as something which, once in existence (whether needing creation from outside in order to get started, or not), goes on existing of itself, independently. He then thinks that any action of God in specially creating and maintaining in existence each human person, or each human soul, would constitute an intrusion from outside into an otherwise independent universe. He does not realise that the whole universe and each thing in it, even the merely physical and material, depends for its very existence and continuance on God's constant action. As Thomas Aquinas explains it: as light is not rooted in the air, but ceases when the action of the sun ceases . . . so the existence of things depends upon God . . . as the air would lose brightness if the sun ceased to shine, so things would cease to exist apart from God's constant activity. And in giving things existence, He gives each thing existence according to its nature: material things existence as material things; persons existence as things transcending the merely material. So, His action in giving to human beings a kind of life which transcends the powers of the merely material to produce is

14

not an irregularity or an intrusion into a sphere from which He and His actions are otherwise absent, but a part of His acting towards each thing in the way appropriate to it, in this case giving extraordinary dignity to the human act of co-operating in procreating new human beings.

So, this personal existence and life which He accords to human beings is His gift. We co-operate in its inception, but it is outside our power alone to bring into or to maintain in existence, and outside our competence or authority to take away—unless, God having constituted man a social being with will, such a man wilfully breaks the bonds of society, removing the absolute bar to taking his life if preventing or punishing his harmful action requires this taking of his life as part of protecting the common good.

This, then, is the chief wrong, from the theistic and Christian view-point, in the taking of human life. It is a usurpation of God's authority in respect of innocent life; it involves ignoring the role of God as agent in creation; it involves pretending or supposing there to be only two parties, not three, involved in procreation, and only one in suicide. (Indeed, this is the background of regarding abortion as irreligious right from conception, even if there be a stage in the first two weeks or so after the conception when the embryo or conceptus is unformed or not a unitary organism. It would be irreligious even then, because the whole blueprint for a new human being is even then already set, and set towards development to human personhood, in such wise as to depend only upon a development according to nature, not upon any new human intervention or distinct act of co-operation. God's agency and providence enfolds the whole process and has already proceeded beyond the stage which depends on man's initiatory co-operation.)

And when God gives human life, He gives a life which of its nature is such as to unfold and develop psychosomatically and in gradual stages. If at some point we say, "we can cut the life off close to its root, without thereby removing God's freedom to bestow grace and personal relationship to Himself", we are nonetheless casting His gift back in His face, since what He gave was *human* life, a life of its very nature incomplete in its inception and such as to grow to maturity, natural or supernatural, gradually and in a context of earthly relationships and environment, with their mixture of joy, struggle and pain. We are human beings, not angels.

Life is given in stewardship. It is something of which, in its existence and growth, laden with unseen possibilites, God is the primary master, caring for it more deeply, determinedly and fiercely than we, and immediate to it, never absent. This is the context of the active medical and paramedical care to which indeed men are called, but within which they should respect, not usurp or deny His primary lordship and care. The good of human life, as His creation, and His position over already existing life as the primary *responsable*, are today constantly denied.

In paediatric writing, this denial has now become absolutely explicit in the direct attack on God involved in the concept of "wrongful life"; but the same idea already underlies many discussions of abortion (as for social or population reasons) and of euthanasia. This concept implicitly accuses not only men, but also God, of making a mistake, and takes on man's shoulders the job of correcting His work, terminating the life He is maintaining, and whose possibilities are limited only by His providence.

Nowhere is a loss of the sense of life's being a gift, with its possibilities not limited to what we can see or control, more evident than in our thinking of the handicapped, the elderly and the dying. The temptation to despair, to think of oneself as an encumbrance, without rights before God or man, is very strong amongst these people; and today the doctor is invited to agree in this despair and even in effect to co-operate in suicide. For the Christian doctor, this is not only a violation of human rights, but also a betrayal of faith. Suicide and voluntary euthanasia in so far as they are fully deliberate and expressions of settled unfaith represent more direct insults to God, whether in the despair they express, or in the will to seize final control over one's own end, than does murder. The Psalmist, Job, Elijah, Jeremiah, sense themselves as afflicted to the limit; but to usurp lordship over their lives by suicide, in order to escape affliction is totally alien to their mentality.

16

We have come, in our attitudes, to agree with our secular colleagues and co-workers, and with our patients—ever liable to despair, or to think of themselves as encumbrances—in regarding God as an absentee. Awe or fear of God is therefore dead; a few fear Hell as a distant consequence of actions; none fear God in His overshadowing unimpaired immediacy of presence. We fear patients and clients, colleagues, public opinion, the law and the state, and there is no echo in our minds of "We should fear God rather than men."

It is vital in thinking about these matters to avoid bringing the truth into disrepute by confusing things that are different. We have a duty not to commit suicide, but no duty to over-protect our life: the guilt and evil of suicide do not arise merely from one's own death being the foreseen consequence of one's actions, but from its being the end aimed at in one's action or part of the chosen means to such end. We have a duty not to kill (e.g. by direct refusal of natural feeding, when there is no counter-indication, e.g. because of feeding doing harm), but no unqualified duty to take measures to preserve life which would not be taken at home, could not be provided in most of the Third World, and which may represent legitimate uses of private but not of public funds and effort. (I make these remarks because the question of what constitutes an "extraordinary measure" to preserve life is a very complex one, affected by questions of resources and of positive law and custom, but should not be allowed to obscure basic principles and those cases that are clear; see Appendix B.)

17

III

Taking Innocent Life: Inhuman?

I said, secondly, that in Christian understanding the acts concerned were not only irreligious but inhuman. The significance of the *innocence* of the life is evident in the ordinary man's sentiments in regard to atrocities in war: to his horror at the general carnage of war is added a particular sense of the wickedness when the non-combatants are wilfully slaughtered as at Lidice in Czechoslovakia or Domodossola in Greece. But the general question is one of man's attitude to his fellow human beings: is a human being like a motor-car, to be scrapped early or late, if it functions defectively, or do we say that human beings have value in themselves, not only in so far as they function well? And how can we express this attitude of attributing value to people in themselves? The moment that in some cases we move towards taking the life of the elderly or handicapped committed to our charge, we begin to destroy the trust they have in us, or, if it is a matter of their consent, begin to invite them to consider their lives, not as a gift with value in itself, but as having no place on earth—as an encumbrance to others. By reducing vision of what does or might give man's life value to some stereotyped or finite image, we remove the springs of hope when it becomes clear that such limited finite vision leaves no scope for hope. If at some point we say, "thus far generosity, and no further", we then begin to write off, as beyond being worth expending time upon, those who would require more, whether they be infants or handicapped or the aged, and encourage them also to despair.

The moment we allow one plausible reason for taking innocent life, it becomes clear that, as our resources become more and more limited, if it were previously justified in those few cases, it then

18

will be justified in many; and we then start to move towards the "final solution", of eliminating from this world those people who present us with a problem or risk, reducing the number of those claiming or liable to claim our generosity, not allowing them to enjoy even that existence they have, lest they stand as an abiding record of society's unwillingness to live less richly or be put out for their sake. The trouble with those who profess themselves Christians is that we see society as a whole as outside our control, and predict that it will not behave humanly, and that then, instead of letting our non-conformity stand as a witness against society, we are liable to pretend not to be in control even of our own actions, and allow ourselves to enter the role of technicians occupied in limiting the damage resulting from society's policy and from the attitudes resulting from the mis-education it has established.

What looks more human when looked at in small perspective declares itself as inhuman when it is seen as a beginning of the abandonment of any vision which could protect man when the pressures become greater. Suicide seen first as reasonable in only a few cases becomes envisaged as reasonable in many, and in the form of agreement to euthanasia even almost in all. Abortion, proposed first only for the most extraordinary therapeutic reasons, comes to seem acceptable in a vast number of cases, and even as part of a general population policy. Once the vision is lost of a call, invitation, and God-offered capacity for faith, hope, and love, which abides through every deprivation of parental love, every degree of disablement, and every pattern of approach to death, who will set limits to when the deliberate taking of life is to be the preferred option? Once the recognition of human existence as a gift, a gift nurtured and developing amidst a context of mixed joy and suffering, is lost, how is there any limit to be set to when this gift may be set aside and abandoned?

So it is that, while man has a natural insight into the evil of taking innocent human life, he finds it difficult or impossible to remain true to this insight, and to maintain rational consistency in adhering to it, if he loses sight of the religious dimension. The taking of life is inhuman as much as it is irreligious, but as René Voillaume says,

"The hope which goes beyond this world, far from weakening the zeal to build the (earthly) city, is by a strange paradox indispensable . . . man is incapable of bringing to the building of his own city the spirit which alone makes it fully human, if he does not direct his gaze beyond time to the city which is eternal. Unless he looks to this eternal city, the city here on earth becomes uninhabitable." Religious insight is the indispensable undergirding of even that human value which the secular humanist wants to preserve.

IV

Objections appealing to Consequences

The principal argument brought against the position I have outlined is straightforwardly this, that it involves in many cases allowing situations to arise full of bad consequences, consequences apparently worse than would have arisen had innocent life been killed. This argument is further bolstered by the question of what is the morally significant difference between letting something happen (letting a person die, letting a child be conceived who is likely or certain to miscarry) and bringing it about (killing, terminating a life, by an act of euthanasia or abortion), and by the presumption that acts and omissions are only to be judged by their consequences, and all else is irrelevant.

Now, as an academic philosopher I cannot fail to be aware that there are umpteen arguments to show that this view, that acts and omissions are only to be judged by their consequences, is *rationally* absurd—just as absurd for the non-Christian as for the Christian. And if Christians produce versions of doctrines supposedly making love the sole criterion of rightness or wrongness in acts (without indicating how to judge what accords with love), or any other views which result in consequentialism, then this is, for me, as a rational being, aware of the academic objections, sufficient to refute these views. (See Appendix C.)

However, academic argument, alas, moves few. And it may seem to leave open the possibility that there may remain irresolvable conflicts of obligation, left to be resolved purely subjectively, or as society dictates. And though futher academic argument stands against these let-outs, it may be that few will pause to hear and weigh it.

I propose, therefore, rather to ask you to look directly at what is involved in some of the comparisons made. In the euthanasia case, one is sometimes presented with the picture of a hospital ward, in which it is said that a man will certainly die within a few weeks after much pain and mental confusion or large sedation and little human contact or communication with others, or else, if given some pill or injection, will die today without all this distress to himself or others. We are then, further, presented with the picture of the consultant being responsible for choosing which course shall be followed, as being responsible for whether the man dies now or later, as being responsible for when he dies. But this is to misdescribe the situation. If the man is allowed to die, normal treatments being continued but not expected to prevent death, no man is responsible for his death or for its time, but it is the disease, or nature, or God that is to be blamed, whereas if euthanasia is administered in form of pill or injection, those whose action and consent to action is involved are responsible, not the disease, nature or God. To pretend that man is responsible whichever happens is to assume an omniresponsibility in man which he does not have. To ignore the distinction between events following on my action, resulting from concomitant circumstances for which I am not responsible, and, by contrast, things directly intended, as means or ends, in the action itself, is to elevate man to the situation of God. Even the pagan world before Christ could have seen such a pretence, of being responsible for what in fact nature is responsible for, as an example of *hubris* or overweening pride.

In the case of abortion, the doctor is liable to be presented with a situation to which there is no satisfactory solution: none of the options, the single parent life, the bearing of the child later to give it for adoption, abortion, is "satisfactory". But society pushes the problem at the social work and medical professions, saying, "Solve this problem or bring it to a tidy issue: take responsibility for what occurs". Again, man is being invited to *hubris*, the pride or arrogance of assuming a responsibility and capacity which he does not have. The Christian must support the pagan in rejecting this pose or role of omnicompetence or omniresponsibility.

22

Sometimes the issues are obscured because men have at some earlier stage assumed some larger role than they need without realising the consequences. Killing may be achieved by omission as well as by commission, e.g. by means of omitting natural feeding. However, if by extraordinary measures, e.g. intravenous feeding, we succeed in preserving life, then we have obligation to the person whose life we have preserved, however handicapped or dysfunctional he or she may be. Society or individuals can be inconsistent, going beyond obligation in providing resources to preserve life, which in the normal course of nature would have passed to a natural death, without providing the continuing care and love due to such a life, if preserved. The solution is not to envisage taking life after it has been officiously preserved, but to be responsible in considering its preservation.

The pagan world could see the possibility of *hubris*, when man vaunts himself above nature and assumes a station which is above the human—but for a Christian or Jew, this should be seen as having another aspect. The tendency of man to assume responsibility, not to the limits of his nature and station, but beyond this as if he were the only responsible agent at work in the world, involves a denial of the doctrine of God's individual providence. Conversely, a lively appreciation of God's providence undergirds the proper humility that the secular humanist and environmentalist themselves often recognise that man needs to have in the face of nature. To walk the tight-rope between a false passivity in the situations nature and human society put before us, and an overweening technology in which no limits are set to the tasks, responsibilities, and methods of medical persons and social engineers, is difficult for anyone: it is again a case in which true humanity is not constricted or betrayed, but re-inforced and protected by respect for God and a realisation of the universality of His activity and providence.

One should not allow the existence of difficult or borderline cases to obscure one's judgement about clear cases. Hard cases make bad law, and it is the principles one uses in clear cases that assist one in difficult ones.

V

Christian explanation to non-Christian

What in this setting can a Christian say to his non-Christian colleague? He can point out the absence of rationally relevant distinction between late abortion and infanticide; the unreasonableness of making anything turn on the question of viability; and the arbitrariness of any setting of a time to viability; he can point out the effects upon society (a) if old people come to think of themselves primarily, not as people, but as encumbrances, and (b) if old people come to think of hospitals and doctors as places and people occupied in doing people away; he can above all try to undermine the arrogance or *hubris* which assumes responsibility over what is not man's responsibility but nature's or God's, and insist upon, both for the doctor and the social policy maker, limits to the types of role and responsibility they are supposed to assume, weaning their colleagues from more general or arrogant conceptions. With his colleagues his situation is in one way easier; he can negotiate, and sometimes command, sometimes comply with command, sometimes not comply. With his patients or clients with whom he is in a counselling and serving role, but with limited energy resources and time, his situation becomes more difficult, the more he is involved. He can alert people to risks to their own health and fertility; he can alert people to the question whether they are making future happiness depend upon a pretence or lie, e.g. the pretence that it is not human life that has been taken, or that nothing comparable to infanticide or to murder or suicide is or has been involved. But beyond this it appears that either he must avoid too much involvement, or he must be prepared to meet with or perhaps discuss issues involving hope and despair, and questions as to what human life is and is about, and even about God. What he can never rightly or rationally do is pretend to be a mere technician, and pretend not be to be responsible for what he does in fact himself do.

VI

Christian appeal to fellow Christian

What then should a Christian say to his or her fellow-Christians when they disagree with the position handed down to them, held by their forefathers as a datum of God-given law? They can point out that if there is a commandment not to kill in the Scriptures, and if reason suffices to see that there is no relevant difference between abortion and infanticide so far as the taking of human life is concerned, it is improper to think that there needs to be another commandment before a Christian recognises abortion as against God's commandment.

Further they can point out that, although Scripture recognises many cases of morally permitted killing, in punishment, or in police-type action, the commandment leaves no room for the taking of the life of the innocent, unless it be at God's directly revealed individual, explicit, command (limited to some Old Testament cases as with the command to Abraham in respect of Isaac). It cannot be said to exclude only "murder", or only "unlawful" killing, *if* these be defined in terms only of the codes of law and custom in this or that particular society (a peculiar interpretation put forward by Revd Dr R. F. R. Gardner in recent times). They can point out that, though it may be consistent for a materialist to say there is only a difference of degree or of importance between a supposedly pre-human, non-personal, early stage embryo, and a fully-fledged human person, it is not open to the Christian to say this: at each stage, either there does already exist, or there does not, a being with henceforth unending existence, for good or ill, in relationship to God. If he says that relationship constitutes personhood, then to be created by God with by nature an unending existence, enfolded from the start by His providence, is a relationship and suffices to constitute us persons, even if we be born bereft of human parental love. True, there is a significant human query as to when abortion becomes murder and therefore becomes a wrong not only against God, and against parenthood, but against an actual child. This is the query when the embryo comes to be as an actual human person, e.g. whether from conception or whether from two or more weeks later. However, this query makes little difference from the point of view of the Scriptures, which envisage Jesus' human life as starting when Mary was first pregnant, and which when they envisage God's providence as active in regard to Jeremiah and John the Baptist in the womb are merely instancing what is more eloquently stated in Psalm 139: 13, "For Thou didst form my inward parts, knit me together in my mother's womb", and its context.

A Christian speaking to his fellow-Christians can fortify them with the thought that in this witness they are not in a minority amongst Christians. Elisha prayed to God to open the eyes of Gehazi, so that he might see that "they that be with us are more than they that be with them"; and, if we but open our ears to the word of the Spirit to the Churches, we may be aware of the Christian community over all the ages, its members both simple and intellectual, agreed in this tradition of respecting innocent life: just as indeed the medical profession, again with traditions supra-national and supra-temporal, has in the past exhibited a similar unanimity, most strongly reaffirmed in 1948 at Geneva. We are primarily human beings, whose citizenship is in a company bestraddling time and space, and the loyalties both spiritual and natural that spring from this take precedence over any local or national laws. We know that in former times, and even now in other places, Christians have been strongly pressed, so that some professions have been closed to them, or only open to them at the cost of non-compliance at some points. There is no reason to expect our society, which has as strong a tendency to believe the world self-sufficient and self-contained as any Marxist society, to remain free from such situations.

27

Nothing I say is easy: in complex situations of counselling and of action, a Christian may be uncertain whether he has made the right judgement or a mistaken one, and uncertain whether if the judgement were mistaken, it was a mistake made in entire good conscience, or made in mixed conscience under pressure. An example of these doubts could be, say, a GP who is involved in counselling and in various questions as to whether, how and to whom, to refer people seeking abortion. Here, if his central commitment to God and belief in God's immediacy and providence is untarnished, he will be capable of detachment in thinking about whether some of his previous judgements were mistaken, and less disturbed by the question of the degree of his good conscience in making them. And, for Christians perplexed by therapeutically difficult cases, there is a difference between on the one hand their closeness to us, if they are occupied with an ongoing struggle amidst perplexity nonetheless to remain true to the principle of the God-givenness of life, and on the other hand their effective abandonment of this principle.

But it does appear that there are areas of social work and medicine, not only gynaecology, but also psychiatry, anaesthetics and general practice, to which Christians are indeed called but, if thus called, then called to a life of nervous strain because of involvements with colleagues and patients and clients, and perhaps sometimes to a life involving partial renouncement of promotion in career. In this context the thought of René Voillaume, Prior to the Little Brothers of Jesus, seems peculiarly applicable: "In an age in which man is persistently and brutally confronted with his destiny, I am convinced that the contemplative life [he has explained this as meaning personal religion based on the prayer of attention and adoration] is called upon to be diffused more and more throughout Christianity. There are circumstances in which the Christian believer can find himself cornered: he feels he must either become a contemplative or cease being a Christian. Today we are, I believe, at a stage in the growth of the Church which will take the form of a much more deliberate and more universal diffusion of contemplation throughout the entire Christian people.''

APPENDIX A

Early Christian Documents

Since the beginning of her history the Church's pastors and teachers, from the early Fathers onwards, taught the same doctrine. The varied opinions on the infusion of the soul did not introduce any doubt about the wrongness of abortion and infanticide. We give here representative selections of documentation from the earliest centuries of the life of the undivided Church.

Part One: The East

1 THE TEACHING OF THE TWELVE APOSTLES
or THE DIDACHE PROBABLY FIRST CENTURY AD

It was previously thought that this document was written about AD 150; it is now commonly considered to be contemporaneous with Saint Matthew's Gospel. It begins:

> This is the teaching of the Lord
> through the twelve Apostles:
> There are two Ways,
> the one is the Way of Life,
> the other is the Way of Death,
> and there is a great difference
> between the two Ways.
>
> This is the Way of Life:
> First, you shall love God who made you,
> secondly, your neighbour as yourself;
> and whatever you would not like done to you,
> do not do to another . . .
>
> The second commandment of the teaching is:
> You shall not commit murder.
> You shall not commit adultery.
> You shall not commit sodomy.
> You shall not commit fornication.
> You shall not steal.
> You shall not use philtres.
> You shall not kill the child in the womb
> or murder a new-born infant . . .

2   THE EPISTLE OF BARNABAS PROBABLY
    END OF FIRST CENTURY AD

3   THE EPISTLE OF DIOGNETUS SECOND CENTURY AD

4   ATHENAGORAS OF ATHENS: THE SUPPLICATION
    ON BEHALF OF CHRISTIANS AD c.177

A passage in The Supplication on behalf of Christians *written by
Athenagoras of Athens shows the struggle that primitive Christianity had in
defending the right to life of the unborn and the new-born. According to the
Roman law of the time the foetus had no protection against parents bent on
infanticide:*

. . . We say that those women who use drugs to bring on abortion
commit murder and will have to give an account to God for the
abortion . . . For it does not belong to the same person to regard
the very foetus in the womb as a created being and therefore an
object of God's care, and when it has passed into life, to kill it;
and not expose an infant because those who expose them are
chargeable with child-murder, and on the other hand, when it has
been reared, to destroy it. But we are in all things always alike
and the same, submitting ourselves to reason and not over-ruling
it . . .

5   CLEMENT OF ALEXANDRIA:
    CHRIST THE EDUCATOR AD 195

But women who resort to some sort of deadly abortion drug kill
not only the embryo but, along with it, all human kindness . . .

6   THE COUNCIL OF ANCYRA: CANON XXI AD 314

*Canon XXI of the Council of Ancyra was ratified by subsequent Ecumenical
Councils.*

31

Concerning women who commit fornication and destroy that which they have conceived, or who are employed in making drugs for abortion, a former decree excluded them (from communion) until the hour of death, and to this some have assented. Nevertheless, being desirous to use somewhat greater leniency, we have ordained that they fulfil ten years (of penance) according to the prescribed decrees.

7 BASIL THE GREAT OF CAPPADOCIA: FIRST CANONICAL LETTER AD 330-379

In his First Canonical Letter, *addressed to Amphilochius, bishop of Iconium, Saint Basil insists that God's mercy in forgiving sins depends on the quality of the penance and the sincerity and contrition with which it is performed; not in the time spent in performing penance. He wrote the letter (No. 188 in most collections) in AD 347:*

She who has deliberately destroyed a foetus has to pay the penalty of murder. And any hair-splitting distinction as to whether the foetus was formed or unformed is inadmissable with us. For here it is not only the child to be born who is vindicated, but also the woman herself who made an attack on her own life because in most cases women who make such attempts die. The destruction of the embryo is an additional crime, a second murder, at least if we regard it as done with intent. The punishment, however, of these women should not be for life, but for the term of ten years. And let their treatment depend not on a mere lapse of time but on the character of their repentance.

Some scholars have concluded that since in Canon 56 St Basil imposes a twenty-year penance (exclusion from communion) on the wilful murderer and in Canons 11 and 57 only a ten-year penance on the involuntary murderer Basil considered the woman an involuntary murderer. Other scholars however believe that Basil's view was that the woman was a voluntary murderer but was not subjected to the full penance of twenty years because grave fear of being detected in shame and being punished had led her to the act.

8   JOHN CHRYSOSTOM AD 334-407

(i)   HOMILY XXIV ON THE EPISTLE OF PAUL TO THE
      ROMANS

Why sow where the ground makes it its care to destroy the fruit?
where there are many efforts at abortion? where there is murder
before the birth? for even the harlot thou dost not let continue a
mere harlot, but makest her a murderess also. You see how
drunkenness leads to whoredom, whoredom to adultery, adultery
to murder; or rather to a something even worse than murder. For
I have no name to give it, since it does not carry off the thing born,
but prevents its being born. Why then dost thou abuse the gift of
God, and fight with His laws, and pursue what is a curse as if a
blessing, and make the chamber of procreation a chamber of
murder, and arm the woman that was given for child-bearing unto
slaughter?

(ii) HOMILY XXVIII ON THE GOSPEL ACCORDING TO
      MATTHEW:

In truth all men know that they who are under the power of the
disease of covetousness are wearied even of their father's old age;
and that which is sweet, and universally desirable, the having of
children, they esteem grievous and unwelcome; many at least with
this view have even paid money to be childless, and have maimed
their nature, not only by slaying their children after birth, but by
not suffering them even to be born at all.

9   APOSTOLIC CONSTITUTIONS: BOOK VII

*These are a collection of ecclesiastical laws, thought to date from the latter
half of the fourth century and almost certainly of Syrian origin.*

Thou shalt not slay thy child by causing abortion, nor kill that which
is begotten; for "everything that is shaped, and has received a soul
from God, if it is slain, shall be avenged, as being unjustly
destroyed". (Exodus 21: 23, LXX)

Part Two: The West

1 MINUCIUS FELIX: THE OCTAVIUS AD 180/92

In fact, it is among you that I see newly-born sons at times exposed to wild beasts and birds, or dispatched by the violent death of strangulation; and there are women who, by the use of medical potions, destroy the nascent life in their wombs, and murder the child before they bring it forth . . .

2 TERTULLIAN: APOLOGETICUM AD 197

But with us murder is forbidden once and for all. We are not permitted to destroy even the foetus in the womb, as long as blood is still being drawn to form a human being. To prevent the birth of a child is anticipated murder. It makes no difference whether one destroys a life already born or interferes with its coming to birth. One who will be a man is already one . . .

3 LACTANTIUS: THE DIVINE INSTITUTES AD 305/10

. . . Therefore, in this command of God, no exception whatsoever must be made. It is always wrong to kill a man whom God has intended to be a sacrosanct creature. Let no one then think that it is to be conceded even, that newly-born children may be done away with, an especially great impiety! God breathes souls into them for life, not for death. Yet men, lest they stain their hands with that which is a crime, deny light, not given by them, to souls still fresh and simple. Does someone think that they will be sparing of a stranger's blood who are not of their own kin? These are without any question criminal and unjust.

34

4   AMBROSE: SIX DAYS OF CREATION AD 386/9

Men should learn to love their children. We find this to be a normal sentiment among crows who form a constant escort to their offspring in flight. Solicitous also lest perchance they may become weak because of their tender age, they strive to supply them with food. They continue to perform this function for a long time. On the other hand, the females of our species quickly give up nursing even those they love, or if they belong to the wealthier classes, disdain the act of nursing. Those who are very poor expose their infants and refuse to lay claim to them when they are discovered. Even the wealthy, in order that their inheritance may not be divided among several, deny in the very womb their own progeny. By the use of homicidal mixtures they snuff out the fruit of their wombs in the genital organs themselves . . .

5   JEROME: LETTER XXII A D 345-420

Some even ensure barrenness by the help of potions, murdering human beings before they are fully conceived. Others, when they find they are with child as the result of their sin, practise abortion with drugs, and so frequently bring about their own death, taking with them to the lower world the guilt of three crimes: suicide, adultery against Christ, and child murder. Yet these are the women who say: '' 'To the pure all things are pure.' My conscience is enough for me.''

6   AUGUSTINE: DE NUPTIIS ET CONCUPISCENTIIS
     AD 345-430

During the Middle Ages appeal was often made to Saint Augustine who wrote as follows in respect of abortion:

Sometimes this sexually indulgent cruelty or this cruel sexual indulgence goes so far as to procure potions which produce sterility. If the desired result is not achieved, the mother terminates the life and expels the foetus which was in her womb in such a way that the child dies . . .

35

BIBLIOGRAPHY

Part One: The East

1 THE TEACHING OF THE TWELVE APOSTLES
    or THE DIDACHE I : 1-2; II : 1-2

GREEK TEXT:

(a) F. X. Funk (1901) *Patres Apostolici,* V : 2 Tubingen
(b) K. Lake (1977) *Apostolic Fathers,* I : 308-312, (Loeb Classical Library) London

ENGLISH TEXT:

(a) F. X. Glimm (1969) *The Apostolic Fathers,* 171-172, (Fathers of the Church, vol. I) Washington
(b) K. Lake *ibid.*

2 THE EPISTLE OF BARNABAS XIX : 5

GREEK TEXT :

(a) F. X. Funk (1881) *Patres Apostolici,* I : 3-59, Tubingen
(b) K. Lake (1977) *Apostolic Fathers,* I : 402, (Loeb Classical Library) London

ENGLISH TEXT:

(a) F. X. Glimm (1969) *Apostolic Fathers,* 219-220, (Fathers of the Church vol. I) Washington
(b) K. Lake *ibid.*
(c) A. C. Coxe (1979) *The Ante-Nicene Fathers,* I : 148, Michigan

3 THE EPISTLE TO DIOGNETUS V : 6

GREEK TEXT :

(a) F. X. Funk (1901) *Patres Apostolici*, I : 399, Tubingen
(b) K. Lake (1976) *Apostolic Fathers*, II : 360-361, (Loeb Classical Library) London

ENGLISH TEXT:

(a) F. X. Glimm (1969) *Apostolic Fathers*, 361, (Fathers of the Church, vol. I) Washington
(b) K. Lake, *ibid.*
(c) A. C. Coxe (1979) *The Ante-Nicene Fathers*, I : 26, Michigan

4 ATHENAGORAS OF ATHENS

GREEK TEXT :

(a) J. P. Migne (1857-66) *Patrologiae Cursus Completus Series Graeca*, 6 : 970, Paris
(b) G. Brady (1943) *Sources Chrétiennes 3*, Paris

ENGLISH TEXT :

A. C. Coxe (1977) *The Ante-Nicene Fathers*, II : 147, Michigan

5 CLEMENT OF ALEXANDRIA:
   CHRIST THE EDUCATOR II : 10

GREEK TEXT :

O. Stahlin (1905) *Clemens Alexandrinus*, II : 10, (Die Grieschischen Christichen Schriftsteller der Ersten Drei Jahrhunderte, vol. I) Leipzig

ENGLISH TEXT :

S. P. Wood (1954) *Clement of Alexandria: The Educator* (Fathers of the Church, Vol. 23) Washington

6   THE COUNCIL OF ANCYRA : CANON XXI

GREEK TEXT :

G. D. Mansi (1901-1927) *Sacrorum Conciliorum Nova et Amplissima Collectio*, 14 : 909, Paris

ENGLISH TEXT :

H. R. Percival (1977) *The Seven Ecumenical Councils of the Undivided Church*, 73, (The Nicene and Post-Nicene Fathers of the Christian Church, Vol. 14) Michigan

7   BASIL THE GREAT : FIRST CANONICAL LETTER

GREEK TEXT :

(a) Garnier (1939) *Basilii Caesarae Cappadociae Opera Omnia*, Paris
(b) J. P. Migne (1886) *S. P. N. Basilii Opera Omnia* (Patrologiae Cursus, Series Graeca, vol. 32) Paris

ENGLISH TEXT :

(a) R. J. Deferrari (1962) *St Basil: The Letters*, III : 21, (Loeb Classical Library) London
(b) A. C. Way (1969) *St Basil: Letters*, (The Fathers of the Church, Vol. 28) Washington
(c) P. Schaff (1978) *Nicene and Post-Nicene Fathers of the Christian Church*, Second Series, VIII : 225, Washington

8   JOHN CHRYSOSTOM:
(i)   HOMILY XXIV ON THE EPISTLE TO THE ROMANS

GREEK TEXT :

(a) F. Field (1845) *Interpretatio Omnium Epistularum Paulinarum*, Vol. I, Oxford
(b) J. P. Migne (1857) *Patrologiae Cursus Completus: Series Graeca*, 59 : 13-384, Paris

ENGLISH TEXT:
P. Schaff (1975) *Nicene and Post-Nicene Fathers of the Christian Church*, First series, XI : 520, Michigan

(ii) HOMILY XXVIII ON THE GOSPEL OF MATTHEW

GREEK TEXT:
F. Field (1839) *S. Ioannis Chrysostomi Homiliae in Matthaeum*, Vol. I : 4, Cambridge

ENGLISH TEXT:
P. Schaff (1978) *Nicene and Post-Nicene Fathers of the Christian Church*, First series, X : 194, Michigan

9 APOSTOLIC CONSTITUTIONS VII

GREEK TEXT:
F. X. Funk (1905) *Didascalia et Constitutiones Apostolorum*, Vol. I, Paderborn

ENGLISH TEXT:
A. C. Coxe (1979) *Ante-Nicene Fathers*, VII : 466, Michigan

Part Two: The West

1   MINUCIUS FELIX: THE OCTAVIUS XXX: 2

LATIN TEXT:

(a)   C. Halm (1867) *Corpus Scriptorum Ecclesiasticorum Latinorum*, 2 : 1-71, Academy of Vienna
(b)   G. H. Rendall (1931) *Minucius Felix*, 314-437, (Loeb Classical Library) London

ENGLISH TEXT:

(a)   R. Arbesmann (1977) *Fathers of the Church*, X : 385, Washington
(b)   A. C. Coxe (1968) *Ante-Nicene Fathers*, IV : 173-198, Michigan
(c)   G. H. Rendall, *ibid.*

2   TERTULLIAN: APOLOGETICUM IX: 8

LATIN TEXT:

(a)   H. Hoppe *Corpus Scriptorum Ecclesiasticorum Latinorum*, 69, Academy of Vienna
(b)   A. Souter (1917 & 1926) *Tertulliani Apologeticus*, Cambridge and Aberdeen
(c)   T. R. Glover (1931) *Tertullian : Apology*, (Loeb Classical Library) London

ENGLISH TEXT:

(a)   R. Arbesmann (1977) *Fathers of the Church*, Vol. X, Washington
(b)   A. Souter, *ibid.*
(c)   T. R. Glover, *ibid.*
(d)   A. C. Coxe (1976) *Ante-Nicene Fathers*, Vol. III : 25, Michigan

3   LACTANTIUS : THE DIVINE INSTITUTES VI : 20

LATIN TEXT:

S. Brandt (1890) *L. Caeli Firmiani Lactantii Opera Omnia* (Corpus Scriptorum Ecclesiasticorum Latinorum) XIX : 603—650, Academy of Vienna

ENGLISH TEXT:
(a)   M. F. McDonald (1964) *Lactantius: Divine Institutes,* (Fathers of the Church, vol. 54 : 452) Washington
(b)   A. C. Coxe (1979) *Ante-Nicene Fathers,* Vol. III : 187, Michigan

4   AMBROSE: SIX DAYS OF CREATION V, 18 : 58

LATIN TEXT:
(a)   C. Schenkl (1897) *Sancti Ambrosi Opera,* (Corpus Scriptorum Ecclesiasticorum Latinorum, 32 : 1 : 184) Academy of Vienna
(b)   J. P. Migne (1845) *Patrologiae Latinae Cursus Completus*, 14 : 123ff, Paris

ENGLISH TEXT:
J. Savage (1977) *Saint Ambrose : Hexaemeron*, (Fathers of the Church, Vol. 42) Washington

5   JEROME : LETTER XXII

LATIN TEXT:
(a)   I. Hilberg (1901) *Corpus Scriptorum Ecclesiasticorum Latinorum*, Vol. 54/5, Academy of Vienna
(b)   J. P. Migne (1844) *Patrologiae Latinae Cursus Completus*, Vol. 22, Paris

ENGLISH TEXT:
(a)   F. A. Wright (1975) *St. Jerome : Select Letters*, 79 (Loeb Classical Library) London
(b)   P. Schaff (1975) *Nicene and Post-Nicene Fathers of the Christian Church*, Second series, VI : 27, Michigan

6 AUGUSTINE : DE NUPTIIS ET CONCUPISCENTIIS XV

LATIN TEXT:

(a) J. P. Migne (1844/55) *Patrologiae Cursus Completus, Series Latina*, 44 : 432—442, Paris

(b) P. Knoell (1896) *Corpus Scriptorum Ecclesiasticorum Latinorum*, 33 : 619, Academy of Vienna

ENGLISH TEXT:

There is no published English translation of this treatise.

APPENDIX B

Common Areas of Difficulty

Recent controversies make the following further observations helpful.

The use of pain-killers and sedatives

Here, it is vital to be clear that it is the *aim* that is of key importance: if the aim is to relieve pain or to reduce profitless mental disturbance, distress or confusion, the use of pain-killers and sedatives may be legitimate, even if the incidental effect is weakening; if part of the aim or hope determining the treatment is to weaken the desire for food or to weaken the capacity to struggle for life, or to remove the expression of such desire or the expression of distress (such expression as is natural to human relationship and communication) the treatment is illegitimate. A typical and carefully nuanced presentation of Christian tradition is to be found in the address of Pius XII on 24 February, 1957 to Anaesthetists:

"Now the growth in the love of God and in abandonment to His will does not come from the suffering itself which is accepted but from the intention in the will, supported by grace. This intention, in many of the dying, can be strengthened and become more active if their sufferings are eased, for these sufferings increase the state of weakness and physical exhaustion, check the ardour of soul and sap the moral powers instead of sustaining them. On the other hand, the suppression of pain removes the tension in body and mind, renders prayer easy, and makes possible a more generous gift of self. If some dying persons accept their suffering as a means of expiation and a source of merit in order to go forward in the love of God and in abandonment to His will, let not anaesthetics be imposed upon them. They should rather be aided to follow their own way. Where the situation is entirely different, it would be inadvisable to suggest to dying persons the ascetical considerations set out above, and it is to be remembered that instead of assisting towards expiation and merit, suffering can also furnish occasions for new faults.'' (*Acta Apostolicae Sedis* (1957) 49 : 129-27, p. 144, Rome.)

Ordinary and extraordinary means of preserving life

Certain means, e.g. natural feeding, are ordinary in all circumstances and, where available, obligatory where not contra-indicated by, for instance, intestinal complication. Thus, for example, to substitute water for milk, or sedate with the aim of reducing the desire for food, are directly immoral. Other means will be clearly ordinary within the context of custom and resources in one society, but extraordinary in another poorer or differently ordered society. Where ordinary means are concerned, the attitudes of relatives are not relevant. Where extraordinary means are concerned, there is some freedom of choice in respect of the giving or withholding of private resources, and a smaller freedom in respect of public resources. Where ordinary means are concerned considerations of prospective quality of life are irrelevant. Where custom or lack of resources (e.g. in times of epidemic, war, or other crisis) render certain means not 'ordinary' or not the 'assumed norm', prognosis may be relevant, with the restriction noted in the next section. Sometimes a false attitude to death (a 'rejection' of it), and sometimes pride in the power of medical technology, generate distorted customs, e.g. whereby it has become customary to direct excessive resources to the extension of life, so that, particularly in hospitals, resources are regarded as ordinary which might better be regarded extraordinary. Where life absolutely depends on the use, for indefinitely extended periods, of extraordinary means, e.g. ventilation or intravenous feeding, cessation of life support may or may not be appropriate, but is not killing. There is an important distinction between uses of extraordinary means expected to be temporary (e.g. in cases of accident), and uses expected or discovered to be permanent.

The area is full of much complication. The fashion for rejecting any absolutes is partly the result of the ignoring by supposed 'absolutists' of some of these complications. However, to reject all absolutes is like attempting to run a car with gears alone and no brakes: reliance on the good sense of doctors and parents alone, without legal controls, may seem reasonable in one decade, but provide no security against long-term transformations in social and medical attitudes, e.g. in respect of the elderly or the handicapped. A detailed exposition of one traditional working out of these questions is conveniently available in LINACRE CENTRE PAPER 3 on the *Prolongation of Life* (available from The Linacre Centre, 60 Grove End Road, London NW8 9NH).

The rights of the handicapped

If any argument for the killing or letting die of foetuses or infants rests upon the allegedly low or negative "quality of life" which they would enjoy if they were to live, because of some handicap, then the acceptance of this argument brings into question the right to life of all adolescents and adults with the handicap concerned.

If after counsel between doctors and relatives or other connected persons, normal measures to protect the lives of the newborn or of the aged come to be omitted, there is the likelihood (i) of this principle of omitting such care being applied to ever widening groups of handicapped infants and aging persons, in gradual shifts of medical and public attitudes, (ii) of the same principle being applied to the handicapped in their teens, twenties or middle life, creating a disposition to distrust doctors and relatives, or to seek private care, out of self-protection, and even generating fears and preparedness for violent if ineffective self-defence, and (iii) of increased pressures on the fully competent or aware handicapped or elderly person to refuse normal care.

45

Human respect towards the dying

The obligations to care for the dying, and so far as possible to avoid unnecessary occasion of distress and to alleviate unnecessary pain, are not disputed. However, for this care to be properly human, appropriate to what is distinctive of human beings or persons as such, certain conditions must be respected. Firstly, the person dying must be enabled to live in a context of *honest and natural human communication*: in a hospital, a patient and his relatives are inhibited by the fact of being "off their own territory", while their attendants (nurses and doctors) may be inhibited by the often authoritarian regime of hospitals and by prevailing tradition and custom, with the result that a person is more completely deprived of *honest personal relationships* than in almost any other context: this is inhuman. Secondly, the person is not a vegetable but a human being with rights and duties. The evangelical advice appropriate in this setting seems well expressed by Pius XII, with reference to situations where there is a serious clinical indication for the use of pain-killing drugs, such as severe pain or pathological states of depression and anguish:

"The dying man may not permit, still less ask the doctor to procure for him, a state of unconsciousness if, thereby, he puts himself beyond the possibility of satisfying grave moral duties, e.g., arranging important matters, making his will, going to confession. We have already said that the motive of acquiring greater merit does not suffice in itself to render unlawful the use of narcotics. In order to judge their lawfulness, one must ask whether the narcosis will be relatively of brief duration (for the night or for a few hours), or prolonged (with or without interruption), and one must consider whether the use of the higher faculties will return at certain times at least, or for some hours so as to allow the possibility to the dying man of doing what duty requires (e.g., to reconcile himself with God). Furthermore, a conscientious doctor, even if he be not a Christian, will not yield to the importunities of those who, contrary to the wish of the dying person, would have him lose his mental lucidity in order to prevent him from taking certain decisions.

46

"When, in spite of the obligations incumbent upon him, the dying man asks for narcosis for which there exist serious reasons, a conscientious doctor will not lend himself to this request, especially if he be a Christian, without having first invited the dying man, either himself or, better, through the intermediary of others, to fulfill his duties. But if the sick man obstinately refuses this and persists in his request for narcotics, the doctor may consent to this without rendering himself culpable of formal co-operation in the fault committed. This, in fact, does not depend on the narcosis but on the immoral will of the patient; whether one procures narcosis for him or not, his conduct will be the same, he will not fulfill his duty. Though the possibility of repentance is not excluded, there is, nevertheless, no serious probability of it, and who, indeed, can say that he will not harden himself in evil?"

In the same address Pius XII also said:

"The Church leaves it to be inferred that the dying are not to be deprived of their consciousness without grave reason. When Nature so provides, men must accept it, but they ought not to cause it except for grave reasons. It is besides, the wish of those interested themselves. So long as they have the Faith they desire the presence of their own, of a friend, a priest to assist them to die well. They want to retain the power of forming their last dispositions, of saying a final prayer, a last word to those assisting them. To frustrate them in this is repugnant to Christian sentiment, even to that purely human. Anaesthesia employed at the approach of death, for the sole purpose of preventing the dying person from dying consciously would no longer be a wonderful expression of modern therapeutics, but a truly regrettable practice."(ibid.)

At a mundane level, not only the fulfilling of duties (organising one's affairs, making a will, etc.), but also a sense of the value of continued life may depend on control and skilled limitation in the use of narcotics: a patient may find, for example, his capacity to continue design or other professional work depends on tolerating some pain rather than resorting to greater drug use. Skill in finding the mean has greatly increased here. (I note here the work of Dr Cicely Saunders and others working in hospices for the terminally ill.) Thirdly, as in the case of any grave and permanent loss or injury, *some* room must be left for some privacy under the patient's own control (though this is only of value in the measure that he or she retains some alert use of their higher faculties, so as to be capable of deliberation, reflection, planning, prayer and so on).

APPENDIX C

On Not Judging by Consequences

The most easily accessible presentations of objections to consequentialism—the view that the rightness or wrongness of acts is to be judged solely in terms of their total consequences—appear in discussions of utilitarianism, which is its most common form:

(1) John Finnis (1980) *Natural Law and Natural Rights,* (Clarendon Law Series), Chapter V : 111-118, Oxford

(2) Peter Geach (1977) *The Virtues,* IV : 91-101, Cambridge University Press

(3) Bernard Williams (1972 and re-issued 1978) *Morality,* 96-112, especially 110-112, Cambridge University Press

(4) Karol Wojtyla (1960) *Milosc I Odpowiedzialnosc,* Cracow; and translated (1981) as *Love and Responsibility,* especially I : 25-46, on treating others as persons, not objects of use, Collins, London

www.ingramcontent.com/pod-product-compliance
Lightning Source LLC
Chambersburg PA
CBHW072040060426
42449CB00010BA/2362